Lake Michigan Scrolls

by
John Dickson

The Puddin'head Press

ACKNOWLEDGMENTS

Grateful acknowledgment is given to these periodicals in which these poems appeared: The Kidnapped Poem has appeared in American Goat; High School Reunion has appeared in Apocalypse; Explorers' Club has appeared in Blue Unicorn; Insomnia and On Dozing During A Poetry Reading have appeared in The Chicago Literary Review; Life On The Mississippi has appeared in The Chicago Tribune; The Ring has appeared in The Cumberland Poetry Review; Rarely If Ever Is The Flame Obsessed, The Courtship Of Whales, and The Funeral have appeared in ELF; The Yellow Brick Road has appeared in Halogen; The Appraisal Of Days has appeared in The Illinois Review; Curse, Double Negative, and Mythical Creatures have appeared in Jean's Journal; The Bird, and The Eye Paints The Mind have appeared in Outerbridge; Pygmalion has appeared in Oxford University Press; Migrations has appeared in Pacific International; The Picture On The Stairs has appeared in Passages North; Self Portrait has appeared in Pikestaff Forum; As It Was In The Beginning, Echoes Of A Native Land, Feeding The Neighbor's Cat, and Good Old Boys have appeared in Poetry; Confession has appeared in Quartet; The Conversation, and The Movies have appeared in Rhino; Bathsheba, and They have appeared in Spoon River Quarterly; Rites Of Spring has appeared in Stone Country; Mysteries has appeared in The Guild Complex; In Fitful Sleep has appeared in The Illinois Review; Aunt Kate has appeared in Whetstone; Still Life has appeared in Willow Review; Marie and Quasi Una Fantasia have appeared in Wire; Layover has appeared in Without Halos

Additional copies of this book may be ordered by writing to:

The Puddin'head Press
PO Box 477889
Chicago IL 60647
708-656-4900

Cover illustration by John Clark
Back cover photography by Vicki Grayland

First Edition

ISBN# 0-9724339-0-2

Table Of Contents

Lake Michigan Scrolls

Feeding The Neighbor's Cat

Like an accomplished thief
I slip the key in the lock
and enter the house of the lone cat.
There is a chill in the stale rooms
a quiet of floor creak and faucet drip.

I begin the game we play
search with mock concern and finally find her
hiding in the jungle by the window
or watching from behind the fireplace screen.
As soon as I discover her the game is ended
and she makes sounds like a distant motor boat
strains her cat muscles stretching
or engages me in light conversation.

There's something about this cat –
the eyes… the way they shine.
I knew a girl who had such eyes –
Felicia What's-her-name… lost track of years ago
but now she is this cat completely.

Sometimes we race through the rambling house
clattering our echoes through the rooms.
If I catch her I flip her over
toss her high in the air
strip her of all her regality.
Sometimes she'll claw or bite and then apologize
grow quiet and sit by me,
looking up with her Felicia eyes.
She knows when I'm about to leave
and disappears, not one to show her feelings.

Sometimes in the afternoon or late at night
I walk past and look at the old house
aware that she's in there waiting
watching from each of its dozen windows.
If only she weren't so unrealistic –
her age times seven makes her barely twelve
and besides, she's locked in a cat.

Insomnia

Lie conscious among the ruins of sleep
before the sky turns pewter in the east
though after-dark sounds of the street have died,
and you'll find a point where pretense fades,
where masks are finally removed revealing
life to be a watery soup.

Nuns in their cells, their brows arched in prayer
might have this sense of all their years returning,
of all their days strung out in proper sequence
with only disconnected memories showing –
Harry in his lion-footed tub
his knees scrunched up to pedestal his head
or Marty's ghost, uneasy in the grave
because they buried him without his leg.
"My leg! My leg! Why must I limp through heaven?"

What force exerts this effect on sleep?
Is it the moon? Or rain? Or deep regret
for disregarded opportunity?
Hold the shell of night up to your ear
and wait for answers to roar like the sea.
Listen – it's you, heavy-jowled you,
neurotic you, moving like a snail
hauling your spiraled loneliness on your back.
It's you gouging yourself with blades of guilt
for words you might as well have drawn on sand.

Gradually the eastern sky grows light
and serious concerns grow meaningless
until soon the time to be awake
weakens the consuming need for sleep
and your world reverts to what it was,
except for memories of distant barking
or sad horizons of an endless train.

The Movies

Bulldozers of my discontent
are grinding history into parking lots
unearthing for a moment ancient coins,
skeletons with knife blades in their ribs
and all my memories of the Bijou Theater.

How we'd wait in line through snow or summer heat
then stand beyond the ticket taker's window
woozy from the cheap cologne, shoe polish,
and salami breath until the rope was loosened
avalanching us across the worn-out carpets
past statuettes of pensive nudes and smiling sultans
and finally whisking us to the balcony
of gilded gargoyles, gum under the seats,
and knowing snickers of unknowing boys
calling each other "man" before their time.

Finally the house lights, the balcony cave dark
and I'd be drawn into a black and white dimension
of the German soldier killed when he reached out
for a butterfly on the barrel of his gun.
Or the beauty unmasking the Phantom of the Opera
causing the entire audience to faint away,
their throats plastered shut with fear.

Often the high-octave giggles and sighs behind me
and occasional shrieks as necklaces were broken
conjuring up episodes of touch and warm discovery,
of angels losing their feathers, then their wings
as they realize love is not all saxophones and roses.
But I'd be distracted by the hands of a murdered man
crawling across the screen to strangle his murderer
or by a train outside in the real world
as it shuddered the walls of the Bijou Theater.

I'd leave looking so dramatic in the lobby mirrors
after two hours spent in the Foreign Legion
or watching old C. Aubrey Smith die in his chair
spilling what's left of his red wine on the rug.
I'd leave unaware of the cordoned-off crowd
waiting like shabby statues for my seat,
drift out of the theater unaware of my legs
of the sleeping pigeons huddled for the night
or the stars wheeling through their orbits –
only feeling suddenly great with courage
as I imagined I was Dillinger destined
to be gunned down as I walked away.

Dead Passion Morgue

I'd driven by it several times
never expecting to go inside
that bleak place, the Dead Passion Morgue –
a rock mausoleum of a building
on the corner of Third and Disenchantment.

Small office but neat and clean –
a compact computer, chromium files
and a beautiful woman dressed in white
but sprayed with Teflon or some such coating
to shield her from airborne contamination.

Soon I was following some hunched-over man
down a ramp that led to the catacomb basement
where all the lifeless remains were kept.
First one drawer and then another
revealed dead passions that weren't mine.
When one seemed familiar I was asked to make
a positive identification, be convinced
that this was the passion that ruled me so long,
that had lived in my blood, almost strangled my voice,
made me pour hot words in Rebecca's ear,
made us fight and shout on busy streets,
then lie on the banks of the drainage canal
while I studied leaf shadows in her hair.

But it lay so still I could hardly tell
that this was the passion that drove me wild
made me roar by her house destroying the night
by honking my love, honking my lust,
that filled me with speeches and serenades
for Rebecca. Yes, this was the passion
that drove me to shout, "I am leaving!"
as though from the peak of some conjured-up mountain
causing echoes to roll through the infinite valleys,
the intricate windings of memory:
"I am leaving...leaving...leaving...leaving..."

But that was that – nothing left to do –
just fill out the forms to advise disposition.
What did I care? Cremation, perhaps.
Anything – just so it never returns.
That was that – nothing left to do
but drive away and try to forget.

Yet even now, as I rush around
I happen to drive past that ancient building
and invariably think of Rebecca,
how we danced in the Halls For All Occasions
and I pulled out a tiny little knife
when someone cut in. How once, in a fit of jealousy,
I threw her corsage out the car window.
I saw her not too long ago
pouring tea at the quarterly Bird-Watchers meeting.
She asked me, with almost classic aloofness,
"I forget – do you take one lump or two?"

On The Road

Now I know how it will be –
I'll catch the midnight bus downtown
where the little burned-out women
send their daughters off to visit
and sometimes tired knots of family
help their oldest boy leave home.
I'll sit behind the stocky driver
as he steers down alley streets
and drives us out to open country,
sit by the window feeling lonely,
part of night and part of morning
flying over rumbling bridges
past the philosophic cows
who stand like statues in the dawn.
I'll watch the cars with empty drivers
race past empty fields and houses
until the flatlands turn to mountains
or familiar turns to strange.

Then, hidden in the night's black
we'll stop awhile at Jellico
all dogwood, balsam, mountain laurel,
southern voices in the darkness
speaking weather, speaking roads
as a figure-eighted woman,
eyes gone hazy, body flaming
looms above me, sits beside me
warming me with body heat.
But I'll sit pretending sleep,
knowing what I've left behind
knowing what they must be saying:
"Where is he? Where has he gone?
Where does he keep the unfilled orders?"
They'll be screaming, "It's not like him!

We can't open his computer!"
not guessing I'm down in The Smokeys
with this burning southern woman
sleeping on the midnight bus.

I'm leaving, leaving, not returning.
We'll ride higher up the mountain,
up till the engine gags for air
and fog blots out the road around us.
That's all the future I can see.
Maybe the bus will turn around
so I can straighten out the office,
but I'll stay there on the earth's rim
floating through fog with the southern woman –
just like sleeping on the bus.
And back in the office they'll all be saying,
"God knows where he's gone this time,"
not knowing how close to being right they are.

The Faraway Place

I'm drawn to a river I've seldom seen
so consistently shaded by overhead branches
and lulled by overhanging moss
that moves in a cadence of slow pulse.
A hawk painted against the clouds.
Magnolia blossoms feeding on air.

Does it flow? Is it wild? Or as placid as grey?
Does it ripple like well-tempered clavichords?
It's a river, so does it really matter?
However you see it is how it is
because once you lie on its grass banks
you'll never quite leave – not completely.
Though later, surrounded by casual friends
who, unaware of their horoscopes,
keep laughing or playing their serious cards
and talking to you as though you were with them,
talking until you finally say,
"Did you see that flash of silver bass
pierce the ceiling of its sky
and startle the day with mirrors of sun?"
And they'll fondle their pendulous wattles and say,
"He's not himself. He's not really here
but off on the banks of his make believe river
hearing some pipe or flute in the distance
threading across the fields."

This river is blue when the sky is blue.
Or grey when it's grey. Or red.
But at night it becomes a mysterious place
as seeds of words sift down through the moonshaft
to bathe themselves in a path of light.
A star is a streak and a sail is a ghost
and sounds that have nothing to do with day
cling to the ear like a brown leech –
the death cry of mice in the owl's claw
or the snake twisting the voice of the frog.
But if you're off in a different place
with drinking friends or a smile-eyed girl
and hear a sound like a breaking bone
or a hole in the throat – pretend you didn't.
Never say, "Did you hear that?"
or explain it as part of the night's song.
Never speak of the filigree moss
or the owl's claw or the words on the water.
Never speak of your private river
that flows in its hidden place.

Life On The Mississippi

We were two boys with a homemade boat
under the skies of a blue May morning,
all set to go down the Mississippi –
lifebelts and fish hooks, tools and sails,
as ready as ever for the long-planned voyage.
But our parents decreeing, "You'd never make it."
Even out on the curbstone or on the grass
as we smoked our frustration and spat like men:
"You're both too young," and "That river is treacherous.
Too much reading... too much Huck Finn."
Their words refused to leave us alone,
weaving webs that held us there.
Wouldn't even allow us the chance to fail.

Soon after that I set sail in my head...
have always kept sailing, sailing the river –
in restaurants with the clatter of dishes
or in offices of unbalanced books –
shoving off in Minnesota,
woodsmen waving, wishing us well...
water slapping... shore drifting by...
passing Swedes shaking ice from their hair...
passing churches where they pray to the cold –
cold their strength and their redeemer.

I float past rivers of brewable water,
float past cows who were born to make cheese,
past hill towns of houses on vertical streets
and shore towns of houses chained to the trees.
I drift downstream in this conjured-up boat
lulled by the rocking of river water.
The sunlight takes eight minutes to reach me,
the starlight several hundred years.
And I'm always dreaming I've run away
though never even thinking of home –
only now that the cold is melting –
that now I'm on the river at last.
I drift to schizophrenic St. Louis –
one side graffiti, the other art.
One shore yelling its crotch obscenities,
the other its ballet, concerts and plays.
One side calls, "Come on up, Sonny."
The other arches the way to the West.

Bargetown to Cairo, Memphis to Shreveport.
Cajun, High Yaller, and back-water white.
I drift past warehouses, levees and docks
down to The Delta and Baton Rouge.
The women smile in their printed dresses.
The men say, "Mon, you come a long way."
And I think to myself how cheated we were
say, "Why didn't we just leave?"

In Fitful Sleep

According to the laws of dreams
if you sit with your drink at a sidewalk café
enjoying the sun and the passing people
and frail young trees that spring from the pavement,
someone will slip away wearing your hat
and all night long you will roam the city
seeking the culprit, whoever it was.
You will often see hats like yours bob about
in rush-hour crowds or alone in the distance.
Now and then shout at a man who is wearing one
but he blends with the crowd or becomes invisible.
When it's finally morning you wake up exhausted.

Or say you are reading in your study
and suddenly there's a knock at the door.
When you open it you see that it's you,
you as you were twenty years ago –
selling magazines, of all things.
You tell yourself to go away
and slam the door in your own face.
When you wake from this dream you think things over.
You really did sell magazines once
and recall the many doors slammed in your face.
So you say, "I shouldn't have been so severe –
next time I'll be kinder to myself."

Or you're off on a picnic with Mary McLain
your beautiful, unresponsive iceberg,
serenading her on your stringless guitar
making up songs that you sing off-key
that arouse her constantly brewing displeasure:
"I love thee, moon of my delight,"
and other antediluvian ballads,
romantic, as only you can be.
Then she shocks you with, "What a lovely song!"
and you notice she's really someone else –
bad complexion, scraggly hair, and humorous knees,
but a smile that works on your chemistry.
You sing together all night long –
some silly Lepidopteran song
with never a thought of Mary.

Curse

I will find you,
seek you out
in a manner worthy of the world's great sleuths,
persistent as a flag that flies at night.

Like a lugubrious hound
I will sniff and rub against things you have touched
or clothes you have worn,
follow you doggedly through all of your days.

When the red flowers hang like a heavy mist
and the frog looks up from his murky pond,
you will have the feeling I'm watching you.

If I'm lost in time and there's no returning,
I will ascend and hover above you
like a huge, preposterous eye.

If you lie on the grass
with your rump stained green
and your eyes overwhelmed
by celestial vast,
I will suddenly, spookily, materialize
and you'll run off bewildered.

When the clouds move off with their leftover rain
and the worms crawl up from the earth to drown,
I shall have clung to your hair
and drenched you to the skin.

When you feel the wind
wrench at the timbers of your house
and it blows through the cracks
like a heavy-voiced choir,
you'll know that I'm almost there.

But there may be times
when varicose branches vein the vestigial moon
that you'll dangle your braids from your desolate tower
and call to me, "Hurry! Hurry!"

Quasi Una Fantasia

How did I love thee? I could name some ways
like roaring around thy house by night
honking loud enough to murder sleep.
Or, just for a casual word or two,
waiting for hours in thy usual restaurant
'til one could hardly blame the staff
for thinking I could be some known offender.
Sang to thee over the morning roofs
or as the moon floats down the midnight river.

Without thee I'm an abandoned farm
with one gaunt horse, his shoes rusting off,
a sheep in the barnyard caked with mud
and eggs in the henhouse turned to stone.
Without thee is a chair I feel cramped in,
food I have no appetite to eat.

But where are we now?
Where, in this cloud-wrapped universe, are we?
Too many times my fledgling words
have flown to thy window sill and starved.
Too many little tables have stood between us,
maybe a guttering candle or a plastic rose
and thou across from me, thy cast iron face,
the sparkling hardware dangling from thine ears,
seeming more like a counterpoised construction
than thy old warm self. More like a barricade.
More like some glowering fashion model
or someone who isn't really there at all.

The Funeral

He always wanted to move on,
jobs and marriage, homes and friends.
Even waited for death as one waits for a train,
looking impatiently down the track
for a bulging dot or a speck of light
and talking as though he'd already departed,
as though he were mentally somewhere else.
Then turning to wave as he climbed the steps
as though glad to be finally on his way.

Now why should I rupture a day's routine,
squander a morning mourning for him,
think purple and black and expensive lilies,
talk to people with lumps in their throats
and drive in a line of cars with their lights on?
I mean, he clung so loosely to life,
not gripping it like a bat to its branch
defiant to the very end
like everyone else, even dogs and cats
fighting off death on uneven terms
like David facing the giant Goliath.

So instead I spend my morning alone
upset by his lack of consideration
saying "Go, then – Be on your way
and leave the earth to those who enjoy it."
But he kept following me around
his voice, a bird in a nearby tree
or the call of a dog across the field,
even a woman's voice up on the hill
until he became completely buried
in every living thing.

Layover

Someone in Knoxville looks like me –
nothing phenomenal… after all,
how many versions of face can there be?
Like snowflakes, perhaps, but even so,
who can say there are no two alike?
Who has photographed every snowflake?
Or every human face?

Three times I've taken the southbound bus –
always different, but always the same.
It reaches Knoxville around about midnight
weaves through streets of slumbering houses,
veers through poorly-lighted alleys,
then rests dark and dormant 'til six in the morning
while I wait in the waiting room, wait in limbo
until just before the sun comes up.

Each time as I wait there, part of the bench,
someone jolts me alive, always calling me Bob.
"Bob! Bob! Where have you been?
Just yesterday we were talking about you.
How's your daddy since Martha died?"
Who was this first one, this creaky old man
with the stiff octogenarian joints?
And who was Martha? Who was Bob?
I gave him a smile of recalling old times
and drifted back to my foggy condition.

A year or two later it happened again.
A youngish woman sat next to me
saying, "Oh Bob – we missed you tonight.
What a wonderful party… you should have come.
Did you stay away because of Ruth?
Was that the reason? Was it? Was it?
Forget her, Bob – she isn't worth it."
Who was this woman? And who was Ruth?
I told her I hadn't seen much of Ruth.
"Don't lie to me, Bob… you were thick as thieves
And don't talk like a stupid Yankee!"
She walked off and boarded the Crossville bus.

A few months ago it was two men –
authority figures in business suits.
One woke me with a nudge in the shins.
"What are you up to this time, Bob,
loitering in this deserted station?
If you value your job get to work on time.
No more of this nonsense from now on."

If I ever get tired of being me
I may go to Knoxville and start being Bob,
do a few good deeds to patch up his image
or talk with a drawl and look up Ruth.
Or if it turns out he's died by then,
I'll be Bob freshly returned from the grave
and maybe set off a whole new era.
After all, what's life without some sort of mission?

The Picture On The Stairs

Our long-gone relatives, so grandparently severe
frozen in holy matrimony, glaring from the wall,
so made of rock, stern and craggy
back in those old brown picture days.

How had they met? The glance of an instant,
once-in-a-lifetime thing for both of them
on a ship bound for America? Or maybe she lived
three farms and several hours away –
the strength he drew from and outlived,
his eyes gone watery from love and age.

Or did he choose her as though she were on auction,
checking eyes and teeth and breasts and rump
to fulfill his plans for staunch-thighed daughters
and sons of firm resolve?
Or perhaps it was she doing the stalking
as though she were choosing a special hybrid seed
for the kind of soil she had.

Maybe they were disenchanted or estranged,
he with his closets of mistresses and little crimes
kept separate from his robe and pipe and slippers,
she with her secret lover giving her courage
to play her role of sitting at the table asking,
"Would you like some sugar?"
"Will you pass the cream?"

Or were they rooted deep in church,
welded together by cross and testament,
their mating more sacrament than pleasure?
Though surely one or both of them
passed down to me some of the blood
that must have driven them through their lives
with all the blind possessiveness of animals.

But we've come to ignore them,
rush down the stairs and never see them,
locked in their vanished century.
Roots should be buried, packed in boxes
in the attic and out of sight – not on the wall
glowering at the way we live our lives.

In Memoriam

Ah, floosie of my delight, I hope you're satisfied,
kicking the bucket the way you have,
leaving me stranded here among the tedious quick,
leaving me standing here on this slowly warming planet
speeding through space for who knows where?
Though none of its billions seem overly concerned.

This world is not the same without you –
your humorous legs, balloon-shaped knees
and faraway, lost eyes, because
now only the aura of you, the atmosphere of you
permeates our private spot by the canal
under the clattering catalpa, over the murky stream
where fascinating beetles walk on water, a Biblical
trick they may have learned just by having faith.

Actually the universe ended long ago
but it takes awhile for space changes to register.
Still, the world muddles through somehow –
always some romantic couple dancing 1-2-3-kick
deep in shady pockets of the Starlight Lounge.
Even your landlady and her lover sit at the kitchen table
muttering *Dominus vobiscum* over her pet chicken
as they absent-mindedly play kneesies.

Since you left us for the Great Beyond
there's the sound of muffled tangos, ragtime,
or pavannes hanging over me. Call it head noises
or some cheap radio several city blocks away.
Maybe just a fantasy, a symptom of bereavement,
not that I care that much for things ephemeral
but I can live with it since I'm convinced
it must be caused by you.

Bathsheba

Bathsheba, dressed in gauzy lace
stretches at her apartment window
as he in his stalled train
sits through infinity watching her

saying, "Behold thou art fair, My Love.
Thou hast dove eyes within thy locks.
Thy breasts are like two young roes
that are twins and feed among the lilies.
Honey and milk are under thy tongue."

But it is Ulysses, not David, who sees Bathsheba
and the window beside him is shut
so she hears none of his praise for her –
Ulysses chained to the mast of his routine,
the passengers in the car around him
all with headphones on their ears –
no one hearing his crying out.

And every morning after that
or evenings, as his train goes by,
he looks for her at the window.
Even years later when her building
is empty and abandoned he looks for her.
Even after it's torn down and gone
without a brick remaining he roars by
along his constant path searching for her
mumbling, "Thou art fair, My Love.
like to a young roe upon the mountain of spices."

But she is never there.
Only the train speeding by with its passengers,
their headphones finally removed from their ears,
all smiling at the fool Ulysses.

Mysteries

Uncle Bernard, U.S. Navy, Retired,
sits out in the yard on a make-shift bench
wondering why his toes still itch
on the leg that was once blown off at the knee
and tossed overboard with the galley waste
to feed the fish that prowl the deep
when he served at sea on a Victory ship.
And why it is, in his bed at night,
it seems that his wife is beside him there
with her long dark hair and her soft warm thighs
invading his dreams, interrupting his sleep
when everyone knows she's long since gone,
buried somewhere with perpetual care
and a marble stone, leaving him alone
sitting there in the yard on a bench in the sun.

And why does his son, who comes to visit,
have a leg like his leg that was blown off
and is now just a bone on the ocean floor?
And why does his daughter, who sits nearby
have long dark hair like his wife once had
and looks like her, and has in her eyes
the soft warm love that belonged to his wife?

And sitting there on this bench in the yard
Uncle Bernard, with the sea in his eyes,
wonders about his absent love
who, like the toes that are long since gone,
has never really been gone at all
but lies at his side at night until dawn.
And he thinks about immortality.

Double Negative

In the anti-world of anti-men
    lives an anti-man like me
who sings his plaintive anti-song
    over his anti-tree.

Its branches, spreading underfoot,
    are gripped by the solid air,
but its roots sway gently in the loam
    up in the earth somewhere.

He plucks the strings of his anti-harp
    that is dry from the anti-dew
and sings of his love for an anti-girl,
    the antithesis of you.

Her concave chest and her ingrown hair
    he longs for, more or less,
but mostly he longs for her anti-no
    which she always pronounces "Yes."

The Conversion

Who knows at what age one turns human?
There I was, twelve, give or take,
looking through a knot hole in the wall
of the women's beach house shower shed
having my delinquency contributed to
by startling gyrations of Miss Henshaw
bumping and grinding, luxuriating in the
jets of water that sprayed and played on her,
shaping, thereby, my eternal memories
of provocative, glistening Miss Henshaw.

An experience like the blinding light
that completely converted Paul to Saint
as he long ago traveled the road to Damascus.
But the die was cast by that rash act!
My penalty for peeping through that shower room
knot hole persisting through the years leaving me
equating Miss Henshaw with works of art – The
Birth of Venus, Susannah At Her Bath, September
Morn and The Garden of Earthly Delights,
or conjuring her up when reading Walt Whitman
who moaned of his "aforefelt wonder of women."
But if Miss Henshaw should suddenly appear saying "Hello,"
I would blush, as her clothes turned to cellophane.

In time some synapse of the brain grows vague
and a few cherished memories slip off to oblivion
leaving us feeling a strange emptiness.
Because there have been times of disenchantment,
of reliving the past with long-time friends
dredging up names of teachers we had
but who, by now, have quietly disappeared
in soupy nursing homes or Teachers' Great Beyond.
Of course Miss Henshaw's name invariably comes up
and I, without thinking, will half dreamily say,
"A beautiful woman… beautiful"
drawing jeers from those who never knew.
But I always smile and understand –
that things look better through a knot hole.

As It Was In The Beginning

The end of an era – Miss Grogan is dead!
Wreaths on the doors and the sky hung in black.
She must have reached eighty or ninety by now.
Or sixty. Maybe even a hundred.

If life were a road and the years trees
arching above it from end to end
I would revisit the thirteenth tree
that spreads so grandly over them all.
The school and its bell, the tree still a sapling
and me in the classroom off in space
gazing my fantasies of Miss Grogan –
tossing pebbles up at her window
making her worry about the neighbors
or strumming guitar chords down in her yard
as she voiced alarm about old and young.

Once on a hill that wasn't there
we sat on the grass and looked down on the town
as I sang to her of the body electric –
dulcimer, bells, and tambourine.
Or was it a restaurant where no one spoke
and a candle between us
and me singing songs of her and the cosmos –
psaltery, sackbut, and shepherd's pipe.

Miss Grogan, locked in the womb of stone,
gone to join things that aren't anymore –
teaching me then as she's teaching me now
that living means giving souvenir memories
to everyone who passes by
so they'll laugh when they think of her,
love on recalling her,
hold conversations she never hears.

Od's bodkins, Miss Grogan – the two of us.
If she'd said hello I'd have passed out.
Still, I'd have lain down my life for her –
that buxom old lady, and me thirteen.
She with "What would the neighbors say?"
God, what a laugh. And God, what a life –
a slight whiff of that junky perfume
or the sound of a skirt that rustles like hers
can conjure her up all over again.

Some of her students are smiling inside
and some, with their old November faces,
have lost her in their varicose brains
as they walk with a hobble in their walk,
their coins growing colder in their pockets.
But I still talk to her once in a while
and say what I felt like telling her then –
that she'd always be part of my future.

Aunt Kate

No pictures of her ever hung on the walls.
All that remains are some front porch stories
passed down by some of her dozen children,
of her so frail and with dainty feet
working her garden and chopping wood.
Her husband never spoke of her,
grew quiet at the sound of her name.

And wasn't he the perfect one,
all strut and swagger and joking around
but not seeming real, not really real –
more like some man who just needed her.
Came leaping over the hills each night
hungry for her and expecting her
to receive his gift of loneliness
and recycle it into life.
How she must have yearned for chastity
each time he came to her moaning "Catherine."

Her children would sit at the table laughing –
the five boys and the seven girls,
some with her eyes and some with her nose.
She told them all they came from God,
let them help her with the garden
and read them all to sleep at night.
Her way of living a sort of religion.
Her way of looking cradling them.
When she died they left as soon as they could
to wander off in their dozen ways.

And what of the man slumped over her grave,
shot through the head by the gun in his hand
before the grass had a chance to grow?
Kirk or Curt or something like that
she hadn't seen since before she was married –
came all the way from Farley to shoot himself,
something to keep the gossips warm.
No one had ever seen him around –
not her friends or her children
and not her husband, though after that
he did precious little strutting about.
Rather quiet after that.

Migrations

Each time we moved we'd take the grand piano
have it moved, that is, its three legs amputated –
great mahogany behemoth wrapped and strapped
in movers' blankets, tussled with and sweated over
by two or sometimes three direct descendants
of men who built Stonehedge or the pyramids.

We had it with us all its long piano life –
in the gigantic house I've practically forgotten
except for music that rolled through its rooms.
And in the smaller house where I grew up,
the house where people walking by
slowed down just to hear the music.
Even in the apartment of our forced retreat
where the piano stood alone and hadn't much to say.

Then we kept it in the lobby of a colorless hotel
where men who treasured half-smoked cigarettes
and women always wearing purple
stopped by as though anxious to avoid their rooms –
some saying they had owned a piano once,
stroking tenderly its smooth brown skin.

Once a child who asked us what it was
sat down and played a dozen pieces
because a life or two ago he'd played piano.
And one night a concert pianist visited and played
pied-pipering all the tenants from their rooms
to stand enchanted in the musty lobby... listening.

After that cycle ran its course, we moved to a house
bringing the piano again, though by now
it couldn't hold a tune, and you could see
the carpet through its ruptured sounding board.
It took up half the living room,
although we seldom saw it, disregarded it completely
unless the radio played some Chopin nocturne
reviving memories of that evening in the lobby.
Or maybe Greensleeves or Sweet Violets
and we'd recall that kid who'd never played before.
Or maybe La Boheme or Madame Butterfly
and we'd think back how Mother used to play and sing
and play and sing and play and sing.

The Yellow Brick Road

Often my train whips past that school
where generic girls skip rope, tra-la
and future athletes play basketball
and I think of paths I haven't taken,
blocked by failure or my special star.
I recall the past when I was like that,
acting out roles of growing up
and imagine I'm back there visiting,
maybe squeezing in a desk
and feeling my name carved there long ago.
Maybe talking with the teacher I used to draw –
snakes for hair and several missing teeth,
she gushing to see the results of her molding.

But during my imaginary visit
I relive those years that hardly happened,
dying in that desk while dustballs
gathered in the crannies of my brain
and toadstools sprouted rings around me.
At times I'd be lost in hazy fantasies
designed to help escape that teacher
and her schemes to pry me out of childhood,
goading me with her domineering eyes,
making me swallow my tongue when I spoke
while all the perfect girls and geniuses
kept kissing her preposterous feet
and washing them with their hair.

Though I felt I could go anywhere from there,
as though there were some purpose to it all,
as though an assignment on the blackboard read:
        Go somewhere!
        There are things in life you must do!
Though several disguised blessings have guided me –
flunking courses designed to slow the pulse
or fired from jobs that sharpen the nose,
barred from seeing someone's tedious daughter
or being evicted from buildings that soon collapsed.
That may be how guardian angels work.

Explorers' Club

Through days of copper… days of slate
workers chip away, chop away
the fourteen story dinosaur
built by the builders of pyramids,
rip out hieroglyphics and domes,
blowtorch the grillwork… crowbar the doors
the marble and granite and history.
There are several skeletons in the walls.

The eighth floor is a painted jungle –
palm leaves, zebras and elephants
and a tiger's head over one of the arches.
Bright colored stones fall to the street –
agate and onyx, moonstone and jade.
When the tiger's head tumbles to the rubble
it's like killing him all over again.

Jackhammer mornings beyond the office
afternoons of pounding and digging
hacking to ruins the mosaic murals
of men with dog heads, men with bird heads,
men in longboats harpooning a whale.

And then the cast iron wrecking ball
slamming through the rock!
Clouds of pigeons deserting their eggs
the sun shuddering in its solar wind,
the clock in its tower, hands raised in prayer
while the ghosts of old dead and gone members
raise their glasses for one last toast
before drifting off in the dust forever.

Buzz, Buzz

The little town knows what's going on
with the pock-faced man and the engineer's wife.
It peeks through the windows, laughs in the bars,
knee slapping, belly shake, rolls on the floor
because everyone knows but the engineer
who weaves his train through the hazy hills
and over the fields of the high plateau
flushing pheasants from their nests,
arousing roosters from their sleep
so they can announce another day.

He blows the whistle of his train
to signal that he's almost home
not knowing he's giving the warning sign,
that when his far off, lonely call
rolls across the ancient hills
his wife gently nudges the pock-faced man
who has spent the night invading his bed
but now rubs his eyes and buttons his shirt

and steals away as the neighbors peek
and click their tongues and look up at heaven
and snicker behind their hand-covered mouths
enjoying these scandalous goings-on
that have added spice to their wilderness lives,
as though dogwood and holly were not enough
or the pine stands or the river rocks
or the sun on the ridge or the haze in the valley.
Only the train whistle crying at dawn.

Something Missing

Here's how it was –
off to work in the dark each morning,
home again in the dark at night
looking down from my seat on an "L" train
at the dark streets and dark roofs
or now and then puddles reflecting the street lights
because now it was winter when days were short,
when nights seemed endless and all-pervading
just as it's been since the world began.
And each time we'd rattle past Dakin near Sheridan
I'd look down and see that busy night club
where women and men go in and out,
its light bulb sign announcing its name... LA DROMA...
where life is... where living never slows down.

I could almost hear the guitar and sax
and vividly imagine them playing
any piece I cared to hear.
I'll have to go there some night soon.
I know I'll do that... Enough of this dark, dark life!
I'll go there... eventually go there,
maybe dance two three kick.
Light hair or dark hair, who really cares?
Or maybe just sit there, nursing a beer
as meaningful music seeps from the walls
and life goes on around me.

Ah, La Droma, I'll be there! I'll be there!
Maybe meet someone like Laura or Jo,
someone whose face I'll never forget,
soul mates, love at first sight mates,
Ah, La Droma! A turning point in life for me.
So of course the day came, as days keep on doing,
International Ring & Gear's day off,
a day we'd all looked forward to.

Finally taking the "L" and getting off
at a station I'd always passed before,
then walked a block or two or three
as occasional trains roared by overhead
until there it was... La Droma! La Droma!
Though something was different about that sign...
the "U" and the "N" and the "T" were missing!
Laundromat! Laundromat?
Women rushing about with their bundles.
Oh, the world has hives! The world has smelly feet!
I walked away. Who really cares where?
Walked all the way to the next day,
to International Ring & Gear forever!

Winter-Kill

It's the usual spring,
sun turning the soil warm
flies bursting from their eggs
and bulbs having their annual erection.
The dogs are begetting illegitimate pups
and the mouse in the wall has missed her period.

But old Harry sits as he sat last autumn
blending with the rooms and the walls
and the draperies and the unused piano.

He is putting out no leaves
and his branches are cracking from their own weight.
We ask if he's happy here... if he likes it here.
The sun falls on the carpet.
Prints of dog nose are on the window.

We speak to him of pleasant weather... of money
of vanished times and faceless names
but he sits in the unlit room,
sits in the dim light.

We read stories to him
have the young girls dance
or play music they think will thaw his blood
but he responds with his smile of the dispossessed.

We carry him out to the yard
pack rich black soil around his feet
but he's rootless.
We tap a tube in his side and hang a cup from it
but he has no juices flowing.

He stands in the sun facing the field and the cow
brushed by the warm wind
stand by the moon-fed pond
its lights and shadows on his face
but there are no leaves in him.
Men who have lost their minds
in caves of hidden treasure
have the same look as his.

I think the ants have found him
and are methodically hollowing him out.
He seems the same as always,
not unlike a marble statue,
but later in the year
perhaps in September when the winds blow strong
he should be reduced to a mound of fine granules
and large ants
and no hope.

Echoes Of A Native Land

Tell us about Bulgarian weddings,
how the old men sigh for nights that have gone
and women weep for their own disenchantment
as confident bride and wine-eyed groom
are joined until death does whatever it does.
How she, like brides the world over,
though somewhat biased by love, of course,
is ready for ruling or being ruled
while he stands beside her forsaking all others
but dreaming their faces, one by one.
Then the violins and the young girls singing
and mountains of food served by bountiful women –
Turkish halva and baklava
blending with the rose-oil air.

And tell us how sometimes a bride is stolen
by one who must have either her or death
and to hell with her several murderous brothers
who search the hills for his hidden cave.
Or how often friends get the groom so drunk,
that he spends the night as part of the floor.
Or they carry him off to a nearby hill
and gag him and leave him tied to a tree
where he watches the light in his new wife's window
till almost dawn, when it finally goes out.

Or if he outwits or outfights them all,
tell how he carries his bride upstairs
and later that night sounds a trumpet blast
as he drapes their bedsheets from the window
to proudly display its patches of blood.
And the men with history in their faces
and women, unchanged for a thousand years,
tell how they stop dancing their dances
and shout their cheers and dwindle away
through fields of roses, through valleys of roses
that cling to the heat of the summer night.

Friendship

Poor Harry Whatsisname – can't remember a thing.
Calls me Henry... calls me Sam
though we've been friends forever.
He never should have married Sarah.
Or was she Clara? Maybe Vera –
the sort who could drive anyone over the edge.

He lives on a street of identical houses –
little brick bungalows. Door for a mouth
and a window on each side to look like eyes.
More than once he's come home late,
found the door unlocked,
the stairs where they should be.
But the wrong bed and the wrong wife
though it took awhile to tell the difference.
I'm sure it was Harry this happened to
though it could have been Harry who told it to me
about someone from the Starlight Lounge.

Harry was always the smart one in high school
but sad, the way he's fallen apart
so obvious at last year's reunion
when he told of digging under the train tracks
to let the train roar over him
and how scary it was and the nightmares it caused him.
My words exactly – I should never have told him.

Ah, Harry... or was it Larry?
I really haven't seen much of him lately.
He's maybe forgotten the good old days,
maybe even that kind of beer he liked best.
I'd look him up but he makes no sense –
talks in circles, never gets to the point.
As for me, I'll never forget good old Jerry –
we had some great times together.

Black Cats

How lucky the black cat who stays in the house –
fawned over, petted, referred to as "Kitty,"
maybe sleeps in the bed surrounded by love
or sits in the window most of the day
watching the world go by.

But the black alley cat who roams the streets
causes hundreds of superstitious people
to cringe from this omen of pending disaster
should he or she slink across their paths –
worse than walking under a ladder
or having a bird fly at one's face,
guaranteeing such mishaps as missing a train,
being caught in the rain
or being crushed by a falling piano

In time the poor cat could
suffer from a damaged self image –
sit alone and friendless, a black pariah
pondering the "why" of his situation.
How grand it would be, he tells himself,
to live in a house with a beautiful lady
who'd pet him and feed him and give him a name,
let him have a chair of his own
where he could curl up and feel like a king,
maybe let him spend every night on the bed
huddled next to her warm woman landscape
dreaming exotic feline dreams.
Well dream on, you ill-starred cat…
Take your dark aura back to the alley
and quit crossing everyone's path.

The Canal

Not a river that wends its way to the sea,
each mile an adventure, an exploration
that stretches into imagination
if you lie on its bank under one of its trees,
hypnotized by its flow.

It's only a channel carved in clay
straight as a carpenter's mitre box.
Useless to lie on its bank and wonder
when all the while you're aware of its sewage
off to the purification plant,
a sour soup on the way to be processed,
then left in the reservoir to settle –
unwritten songs and failed. love,
ruined wine and forgotten faces
sterile, pure, and dying of chlorine.

A bird that is only feathers and bone,
deprived of its song and mating call,
floats on the surface
along with remnants of tavern songs,
unwanted kittens and unwanted love
all blended with memories long forgotten –
morning sun bringing the farm to life,
steaming streets after summer rains
and walking to school... walking to school.

Canals are channels of liquefied past –
blended with past, a part of the past
that seldom, if ever, reaches now.
Rivers constantly flow to the future,
to the unknown, the not-want-to-be known
away from the dull so-whatness of past.
So now, while the sun is still in the sky,
I think I'll go sit by the river.

Good Old Boys

I've heard the same old story at least a dozen times,
mostly from Aunt Nell when we'd go there for supper,
how Grandad and his army buddy
wandered home from Appomattox
past cow barns and dog bark, pines and moon,
through crisp Virginia mornings and the leafy sun,
eating grits and chitlins in defeated mountain shacks,
Grandad the constant clown, laughing all the way.
How he paid his younger brother to go and fight for him
but when the kid was old enough to join for himself
Grandad made the sacrifice and marched off to war.

How they walked home through the battle-tainted mountains
rich with the rot of shattered mountain boys,
their Alabama accents and Indiana twang –
Dixie mixed with Yankee Doodle in the evening air.
Soft Kentucky voices in the Blue Ridge fog,
their singing sounding ghostly in the air.

Grandad bringing home a fresh batch of stories –
stuck his hat on sticks to tease the crazy Yankees,
or how the captain fainted from horse blood on his leg
then moaning, "Lift me gently, Boys – I'm about done."
Wed a girl from Charleston who loved to hear him talk,
she there in the mountains to avoid the war.
Begat a dozen children who mostly raised themselves
while he told jokes and stories at the mill.

He needed living men to be around him all the time,
not a mulch of country boys sunk in the bog,
men to talk and laugh with or bring home to dinner
and talk all night by the pot-bellied stove.
As they died one by one he stole their army stories
until you'd swear he must have fought the Civil War alone.
Grandad the big hero – a molecule of history
phony as a lead dime, and I'm part him.

Fast Food Restaurant

Princess of the sun and moon
drinks her tea and looks at me
through eyes of oriental slant,
through almost hidden eyelid slits.
The gentle structure of her face –
pink jade, green jade –
hides secrets of ten thousand years
as she drinks her cup of tea
sitting in her usual place
as once she sat in palace gardens,
almond blossom-scented air
foot bridge and cherry tree
a trace of samisen and bells,
the sun pastel, the ground grey
the grass never deep green.
Her eyes are of the ancient East
a peach blossom in her hair
moonlight on the Chinese garden.

Princess of the sun and moon
drinks her tea and looks at me
arousing deepest mysteries
that lie between all men and women,
her neckline is the borderline
of secrecy and revelation.
I know there is no nonsense here,
that I'm Ulysses on his ship
firmly tethered to the mast
sailing past the rock of sirens
who entice and captivate
with hauntingly voluptuous song,
that all the others in the restaurant
are the crews whose ears are plugged
to save them from the deep enchantment
of this oriental princess
who puts aside her plastic cup
and leaves.

Marie

Have you ever sat becurbstoned and wound down
condolenced only by a celibate cat
the color and equivalent of the gutter
while the greatest of all hospitals
looms above you and its squalid neighborhood
much as cathedrals loomed back in the dark
(though maybe cheerier than these) Ages?
Somewhere up there Doctor Whomsoever,
skilled with his scalpel and extremely wise,
is slicing putrefaction from your love
your all who lies, as is so frequently the case,
completely etherized upon the table.

And have you then, perhaps you have,
thrashed about through your befuddled brain
for bits of memory, bits of tattered past
to help reweave that brilliant tapestry
that tells of all your time together?
Those life and death discussions on the river bank
or empty beaches or spaghetti restaurants
while living in each other's eyes,
car-honking coded courtship messages
around her block and by her house at night
and even locking antlers with all competitors
to preserve your egocentric ownership
back in those serious and very basic times
of transmutating jealousy to love.

But now just waiting, sitting there
half deciding that if they cut too deep,
carve out the very spot where life resides,
you'll move away, maybe near some pensive stream
that spreads its gift of life as it flows by,
often startling you with echoes of her face
just to prove how utterly defenseless
you still are against the past.

Then, when traffic sounds and sunset merge
to shades incongruous with knives and surgeons
you get up, abandoning the cat,
the squalor, and all your garbage thoughts
ready to confront the cast-iron nurse
who will convey by eyebrow curve,
hand fluttering to the face, or a pursing of the lips
either that the spirit now has finally flown
or "You may see her now but only for a moment."

The Proposition

Get out of that nerve-wrecking office, Miss Gibbs,
and leave all those papers behind.
Escape this innocuous software life
where just a touch of a keyboard's key
will release a swarm of the world's great truths.
Come with me to a farm near here
where we can lie down with a milk-warm cow
to sleep, perchance to dream of swishing tails
or velvet ears or treacherous bogs of polliwogs,
dream of combines shaving the city streets
as livestock graze in vacant lots.

You'd really like it, thoroughly enjoy
being pillowed by the cow's organic heat.
Like cuddling in the cradle of the world,
throbbing along with that heart-churn engine
and the bellows action of those tremendous lungs,
even the gurgle as silage turns to milk
while being blessed by the sun's cathedral rays
that slant down through the cracks of the barn's roof.
Maybe the goat-hoofed piper on a rock outside
will tootle pagan tunes of wayward sheep.
Or perhaps a star so bright it shines by day
to herald another savior of the world.

Imagine how striking the radiance of your cheeks
or the red of your meticulous nails might look
framed by the cow's brown or the straw's yellow
or feeling your face cool against the cow's warm belly.
And your perfume mingling with her sweet alfalfa breath
as we lie trapped in the giant mirrors of her eyes
that can be traced back to the world's first cow.

When we return, if ever we return,
from that much-needed interlude, our secret may be
revealed by random cow hairs on your sleeve, by some
manure on your shoes, or the scent of new-mown hay.
But only the critical ones of that entire office
will be jealous because only we have sampled life,
or felt the cow's gigantic pulse.
So come, Miss Gibbs, without a second thought,
and sample life, if only for awhile.

The Power Of Negative Thinking

The cat, in its predatory way,
comes up on the porch, sparrow in his mouth.
Big authority figure, his tail swishing
like an army officer's riding crop.
Never wags his tail as dogs do
for camaraderie or happiness or
to strengthen the bond between man and dog.
The cat's swish says what his lope says,
"I am one of the world's great cats.
To prove it, I've killed this bird for you,
put an end to its preposterous singing
and hopping all over your manicured lawn.
From now on you'll think more highly of me
and realize what a great cat I am."

But I say, "You despicable, bloodthirsty cat,"
slap his haunch to show my displeasure
leaving only the dead bird at my feet.
Ah, the poor bird, he'll be missed at home.
They'll grieve at the empty place at their table.
And his wife, how she'll weep in her half empty bed.
I lift the dead sparrow up by its claws,
toss it high in the air toward a clump of bushes
to be rid of it and its memory.
But instead of completing its up and down arch
it revives in mid-air and flies away
leaving me feeling Biblical –
Patron Saint of the Birds, for example,
whose touch can bring sparrows back to life.

Improving The Mind

Guitars sing to her from the ribbon grass,
the moon tugs gently at her tides
and the swimmers call to her from the lake,
but she sits alone, lost in her book
impervious to it all as she reads.

She must be a real live person –
a warm lap and a heart that keeps beating,
but the way she kisses her dog's nose
on nights when Mr. Bancroft comes over
and sits on the davenport aching to touch her –
his arms like vines without a wall.
Frustration glistens on his forehead
as the pennies in his wishing well turn green.

She yawns without even covering her mouth
saying, "Where is my book?"
some highly improbable soggy romance
by someone with a passionate name.
Something has obviously gone wrong.
Has she grown weary of Mr. Bancroft,
of his busy little fingers
underneath the table?
He's as bad as the men at the loading docks,
the ones who whistle as she walks by
making her think of sweaty armpits
and sour breath and hair.

Someday maybe they'll stop their whistling
and Mr. Bancroft will go away.
Then she can sit with the brittle ladies,
lace at her collar and lace at her cuffs,
blink her chicken eyes at the world
and read, read, read.

Self Portrait

Colored birds fly from his brush
he, the creator of flowers and stone
and stars and shells and purple prairies.
Trees spring from the earth he paints.
Bright fish swim from his brush
and the weightless dancing of young girls,
the painful walking of old women.
He, the creator of frogs and doves,
planets dying and eggs being laid.

Why has he never painted himself?
Rembrandt left a history of his face.
And Picasso, Kokoshka and Klee
painted themselves as they knew they were.
It's time that he pause and paint himself.

But he shrinks from the mirror
as he might from lightning or fire in the sky,
as a B-Movie vampire might shrink from a cross.
There are lines carved by his past aloneness,
nights of snare drum and wire brush,
dish clatter in all-night restaurants
or lumpy seats in worn-out theaters
where old Kol Nidre faces surround him.
In the mirror Marie is still in his eyes.
How the wild constellations of her blood
drew him forever into their orbit.
His eyes with the house with Marie inside
still spreading its flames through the night sky.

There are lines from too much saying goodbye,
indelible smile lines from long conversations
with Marie who has hovered inside him for years.

His brush dries hard as he studies the mirror.
Nothing is there in his face he can paint –
maybe puddles of heat on an endless road,
tears weaving their way to a river
or the hopelessness of a treeless land.

He watches the lines of his face grow deeper.
Sailors have faces with lines like his –
their faces sandpapered by the wind,
their eyes curled almost shut by the sun,
their gaze fixed on the rim of the sea.

He chooses a new brush and dips into green
and paints a frail blade of grass.
It is either that or throw out his brushes
and wander off through the studio walls.

Case History

When Miss Simpson took a bath
she would lock the door
and barricade it with a clothes hamper.
The years had played havoc with her gender.

One day she took her bath with no barricade.
The room was a chaos of conquest,
of invaders capturing Roman women,
of maidens screaming as they were whisked away,
but she remained as chaste as Susannah.
For some reason no one broke down the door.

She began taking baths with the door unlocked.
It made her feel daring and full of excitement,
as though she were on the French Riviera
or bathing in some hidden pond.
Her flesh felt younger and more alive,
but the door she kept watching was always closed.

She took her baths with the bathroom door open,
decorously sponging her shoulders and knees.
There was welcome in her smile.
Her eyes were an invitation,
but no one looked in or even walked by.

She had a bath tub installed in the yard
by some plumbers who had never done such a thing.
When she bathed in it, cherubs flew over her,
doves flew about with ribbons in their beaks,
the oak leaves turned silver and tinkled like bells.
One old man looked over the fence for his cat,
and a child stopped by to pick a flower.

She took four baths a day in the yard
and dried off by swinging high in the swing.
Her flesh began growing young and firm
and the sun and wind gave her a touch of beauty.
But no one looked at her. No one cared.

Except five hundred neighbors she'd never seen
who had her committed to Hazelhurst
where she looked through the bars and wore a grey gown
and gazed at the stars and cried out to the moon
and crossed off the days in her desolate room.

But now she's cured and home again.
Her breasts are like feedbags that horses wear,
her buttocks an avalanche of meat.
She has bars on the windows
and only wears grey
and stores old magazines in her bathtub.

The Ring

Long after the others have gone
Maggie works overtime at the office,
her wedding ring all alone on her finger.
The other stenographers live by the clock
and have gone their ways with plans for the evening
while she types the daily report,
her ring reflecting what's left of the fun.

The others talk of last night's dates
or plans they have for their sometime weddings
while Maggie rushes off to the bank
because after all, they'll need baby clothes
and doctors and cribs and books for school
and food and a house and toys and tools
and parties and shoes and money for church
and only Nick will be working then
and it all takes so much money, you know,
but oh, it will be so grand.

The others laugh and disappear,
fly off to the sun, to the sun-kissed sea,
to the sea-kissed men.
They are swept away like pieces of wind
in their ponderous jets that race way,
subtracted from the earth and gone
while Maggie types her reports, clack, clack,
the ring on her finger fading.

Oh, quit and forget the money, Maggie.
You've been with Leonard & Leonard six years.
Leave while your ring still sparkles a little,
leave and get thee great with child!
And if there is no room at the inn,
go back to the barn with the horse and lamb
and the clucking hen and the oogly-eyed cow
and a hole in the roof
where the star shines through.

But she has another report to type
and two or three letters for young Mr. Leonard
and Nick may be laid off again next month
and wedding ring or no wedding ring,
this is hardly the time.

Still Life

The fish, bleeding garlic-flavored butter,
looks up at me from the puddle of his plate.

Fan-tail and fin-plume, a thing of beauty
abandoned by the god of all fish.

The fish and the bottle of wine beside him
are predictions of what the meal will be.

The eye of the fish is still fathoms deep,
when he swam with his kind in an orderly way.

There may be fish memories trapped in his head –
escaping from large fish, devouring small ones,
or sun on the ceiling of his world.

If I'd caught this fish, would I set him free,
feel delighted to see him scoot away
shouting, "Free at last!" in his silent voice?

I would, though always the fate of fish has been
to be caught, eaten and enjoyed –
just as bears do with fish, or as Christ did –
either example enough for me.

Still, were it not for the stomach's demanding,
I want fish to be where they belong –
swimming with schoolmates deep in their world
rather than captured, all hope gone,
in a shallow pond of butter.

Seafood Restaurant

I have seen the observing eye of the lobster
as he looks out through the slit of his armor,
as he waits in the damp of his plate glass pen
to be dropped in a kettle of boiling water
after someone has carefully appraised his size,
the probable texture of his meat
and anticipates his delectable taste.

I have watched him judge the various diners
as they slice up members of his family,
dip their legs into pools of hot butter
and mash them between their restless teeth.

I have watched him study the fat-faced man
and the young woman he dines with quite often,
how he strokes her hand with his buttery fingers,
how she shuns his touch and never speaks,
how they open their mouths for forkloads of lobster –
his steel jaws grinding, she chewing quickly,
her incisors shiny as little daggers.
They finally wipe their mouths and leave
but where else could they go to feel satisfaction?
What could they possibly do together –
he the shark and she the piranha?

The eyes of fish as they lie on their plate
or even as they swim in the sea
all have the same blank expression –
an indication of no thoughts.
But the vulnerable eyes of the iron-clad lobster
are withdrawn and inscrutable, guarding his wisdom –
aware of the future, aware of the past,
even aware of his destiny –
that back in the kitchen a pot of salt water
is gently boiling, just waiting for him.

The Eye Paints The Mind

In the farthest booth of the restaurant's dark
Harry strikes matches one by one,
their brightness glaring from his glasses
and lighting the channels of his brain.

Each one conjures its own illusion,
reconstructing a long-ago fire –
a house wearing its crown of flames
as people rush frantically into its rooms
to save their money or diamond rings
then rush down through the fiery stairwell
with a rescued shoe or a flaming broom.

He is hypnotized by each flaming match,
enchanted by, lost in, consumed by its flame –
a woman at an upstairs window
half hidden by night, half hidden by smoke,
her scream a shred of the night's confusion.
She tosses her child to someone below
but the picture fades as the match burns out.

The burned-out match becomes smoldering ruins –
a timber, weakened by glistening embers,
crashes through what is left of the floor
to become part of the gathering rubble.
Sometimes these fires are followed by rain,
rain that hisses and turns to steam,
arpeggios of a fine drizzle
that become a small cloud, always shaped like a woman
with almond eyes and wild flowing hair
who smiles as she slowly drifts away.
It's then that he ends his striking of matches,
pays his check and leaves.

The Bird

Once on a day like any other
a swift or a swallow, though maybe a thrush,
burst from the fireplace and into the room
fresh from the lazy green of its linden,
the grass of its world, fresh from the yellow
forsythia remnants of spring,
flapping soot from its frantic wings,

causing unusual consternation
because of the rather frightening omen
of having a bird fly into the room
in such a surprising, pantomime way,
strewing ashes onto the chairs
and the table and even the antimacassar
that's been in the family for many years.

Mops and brooms waved like shillelaghs
to urge it out the open window
before it ruined everyone with its spell.
Wings brushing the father's face
meant he'd lose money, or maybe his health.
Circling about their daughter's head
meant her child could be born with hooves
or the mark of the devil on its face.
Oh, the shattering sound of glasses and dishes,
the mother gone limp with her fluttering heart.

And then like hope, like happiness flown,
it found a window and sailed away
diminishing over the grass of its world,
beyond the forsythia fragments of spring
and off to the green of its lindens.

Ben

The Starlight Lounge seems dimmer since he's gone
plucked, as he was, from life before his time
leaving the teen-aged waitresses,
the sap still rising in their legs,
to experience their first bereavement
without a stone to lay their flowers on,
leaving Molly, the cashier,
her tides of smiles and rage ebbing and flowing,
her nails the color of the coins she handles,
stifling her sorrow behind the green lids of her eyes.

While Ben lies scattered, a segment of his eye
sealed in the slide of someone's microscope,
a section of his lung hanging in suspension in a jar
floating like contralto leaves
and lost in a display of pickled parts
that everyone ignores by day
and outlined only vaguely by the moon
a few nights every month.

Ben and his undying reverences for women –
two drinks was all it took and he'd be off with,
"Womanhood, Sweet Womanhood –
I lift my glass to thee,"
talking Irishly or talking Mumbo
grabbing Molly by the shoulders and appraising her,
she and her sweet cushions so comfy to the eye –
the fragrance of her pores
the excitement of her hair enough to flare your nostrils

and Ben looking so sincere and inoffensive
that even she with her temper living shallow in her blood
would smile, turn red, turn almost blue
much like your tightly corseted grandmama
when faced with sexual desire.

O Molly… Molly…
His words soft as heavy snow falling in the dark
soft as a goat bell in the distance,
as the muted mandolining of some blind mandolinist.
And acting the same toward any woman – not just Molly –
those with morning breath as sharp as chicory,
the over-emotional or the emotionless,
either steeped in logic or illogical
for whom the sour armpit was an aphrodisiac. Invariably they smiled at him,
fluttering their hands like statues freed from stone.
Only the indifferent were impervious to his spell;
only the hooded harpies who had not been buried yet.

O where is Ben?
Is his larynx, is his magic voice box sliced and analyzed,
being studied as songlessly as a cat dissects a bird?
And the blood – has it turned to water?
Is Molly's image etched on his formaldehyded brain?
O Ben, off beyond the painted stars,
beyond the ceiling of the Starlight Lounge,
I will visit the exhibit and place flowers on your jar,
go behind the building and lay garlands on your parts.
But next time, Ben, be buried like the rest of us.

High School Reunion

You mean that's Sandy? That's not Sandy.
She was rather pristine back then,
like September Morn on the lumber yard calendar –
one toe in the woodland pond.
Or the topless seltzer water nymph
so chastely perched on a river rock.
Though of course, at times a carrier of books...
graceful dancer... husky laugh.
She was Sandy then, not Melisande,
so easy to be with... not like she is now.
Our year book used the word "Potential."
There were dozens of women she might have become
but never this fortress... no one this cold;
Sandy times three and her smile gone.

But when you consider who she married –
big funeral parlor of a man
born wearing a black suit
and never far from the crow's caw –
one foot in heaven and wearing spats.
In no time at all they'll be just alike,
walk arm in arm through the moonlit halls
and tasteless rooms of their dismal mansion,
through cobwebs that always remain unbroken
and nothing of Sandy in her eyes.

The Courtship Of Whales

Out beyond the harbor mouth
where moonlight flecks the choppy water
the bull lurks just beneath the surface
singing his subaqueous song
of nearby stars and distant cliffs
until slowly, ever so cautiously slowly
she, acting cowlike curious,
looms into sight from the deep sea murk.

What begins as a casual game of tag
gradually turns into serious business –
thrashing tons of leviathan foreplay.
They caress each other with their flippers
ever so gently, ever so tenderly.
She brushes against his pectoral fins,
he playfully nips her waving flukes –
each aware of the other's erogenous zones.

They stroke the length of each other's body
caressing and slapping with their flippers,
brushing, butting, and nuzzling each other.
Then, without benefit of clergy
and quickly, in a matter of seconds,
they consummate their fierce intent.
Now it is she who sings her song,
piping sounds of satisfaction,
before they drift away together –
two silent submarines deep in the sea.

Rarely, If Ever, Is Flame Obsessed

Flame swings on her front porch swing
thinking how nice this hot summer night
while Moth peeks craftily through the bushes
or keeps dashing by on his bicycle
knowing she must be amazed at his speed.
Falls on some gravel or hits a tree
and limps off convinced she's unwinnable.

Gets back with friends doing mothly things –
basketball, swimming, lifting weights
but all the while thinking only of flame,
how beautiful swinging in her swing
thinking of him, waiting for him,
her eyes like a melancholy dream.
Soon his thinking drifts into talking,
braying his love for "this Flame I know..."
the flare of her hair, her flickers of laughter,
fingertips, earlobes, bodice and face.
Her voice and its valleys make him dream,
fill him with visions of her in loose silk.
Her taper of thighs. A bungalow on Primrose Lane.
But they say, "Moth, she's not really for you."
"Dump Flame!" "Forget Flame!"

Eventually marries a colorless moth
grey in her ways and dust on her wings
who cooks the same thing every night –
never truffles or fritters or crepes.
But he still drives by Flame's homey house
in a car with white-walls and chromium spokes,
peeks through the bushes now and then
and finds she's as beautiful as ever
in her kitchen of copper molds and spice,
braised beef and mushrooms in the air.
At night pretends it's Flame he sleeps with –
of all God's moths, the most foolish.

Pygmalion

On the earth in its act of quietly spinning
with its dazed cargo of puzzled people,
half of them sleeping, half of them not,
there can be heard the sound of tapping
from a ground floor window of the Greenwood Inn.
Pygmalion sculpting, fashioning, tapping,
freeing someone or something from the stone,
from the huge rock he's brought into his room.
So far, a rough roundness at the top
and a definite narrowing halfway down.

On a night of flapping catalpa leaves,
a distant guitar strumming its anguish
as ten point seven dogs per hundred
keep baying at the moon
there is still the tapping, tapping, tapping
coming from the Greenwood Inn.
Now the rock has a hint of head with stone hair
almost tumbling onto its possible shoulders.

And on a night of tangible quiet,
of werewolves leaving tracks in the snow
as they hide behind, peek around, various tree trunks,
there is still the sound of tapping… tapping…
coming from the Greenwood Inn
where this graceful woman with sturdy arms
and faraway eyes and the hint of a smile
stands up to her waist in stone
while he, bending down, keeps chipping away
at what could become a thigh and a knee.
He is working compulsively, driven as though
he is certain to run out of time.

On a morning of sun chasing clouds from their puddles,
not a sound can be heard from the Greenwood Inn,
not the clatter of catalpa leaves
nor chipping sounds from the open window,
only a now-and-then flap of its shade
that echoes through the empty room.
The only signs of recent life
are two sets of footprints that lead to the door
through a heavy layer of rock dust.

They

They know he's seen that woman again
by the way he keeps staring off at nothing
and how his sentence endings fade
from thinking about his new-found love
of the weird shape and raspy voice,
her perfume sharper than citronella
and animal skins around her neck.

He sits in the midnight oil of his room
dreaming the rustle and swish of her,
sits in clattering all-night restaurants
of tired endomorphic faces
or in cocktail lounge piano bars
sketching her smile on paper napkins...
and her eyebrow arch
and the slow slope of her shoulder curve,
sits in the murk of all-night movies
or walks through the empty financial district
shouting her name at the Federal Reserve
to hear it echo across the street.

They say, pull yourself together, you fool.
Is this what you want – some burned-out woman
with silver eyelids and lacquered nails?
She must be ten years older than you are.
You can say goodbye to the old fire
when her hands shake and she's dry as a leaf.
Besides, she's always with someone else –
some giant ox with no neck.
We've seen him – the man has no neck!

The leaves drip like off-beat clocks
and the blind trees feel the cool night air.
He tosses pebbles at her window
too lightly to penetrate her sleep.
Soon slowly, slowly, the sad sky of morning
wrenches away from the hidden horizon.
Then he walks up the walk that leads to her door
and stands there awhile intending to knock
but they watch him from the windows and rooftops
so he hates himself and goes away.

How To Write A Poem

There is a need for ritual in our lives –
the fork and spoon always where they belong
and each night the pillow just so high.
Even the dog so repetitious in his ways,
that his paws wear ruts in the concrete alley,

And there are special rituals for writing poetry,
the burning of a young poem in a dish,
and praying as the smoke of it curls skyward
or, dressed as a toreador and gripping
the sharpened pencil like a sword,
kneeling in silence before the sacred shrine
to seek guidance in the coming struggle.

Often one must go to some café
where the soul (we'll call it that)
prefers to live and, as Jacob with the angel,
wrestle with it all night long demanding,
"Surrender it! Release that poem to me!"
And sometimes, by morning, leaving victorious,
thinking, "Now my name is Israel."
Not too far removed from acts of love,
each time death a little closer,
wondering if this poem will be the last.

Sometimes one must hunt and trap the poem,
walk for miles or wait hours or days
maybe find it hiding in a strain of music
or in the lines of an old discovered face,
or the sound of voices through an open window
or in amazing landscapes of the morning waitress.

Sometimes frustration says, "Who gives a damn?"
It's then the poem appears, almost apologetic,
and to make up for playing this silly game,
tumbles from its hiding place, dumping
its entire bag of words out on the page
like the slashing of a sack of wheat
or snipping a packed brassiere.

Only rarely does the question "Why?" arise
but if it does, pass it on to someone else,
an artist who draws in sand, perhaps
a watcher of birds or a climber of mountains
or a highlander serenading with his bagpipes
the empty forest or a fog-bound lake,
to anyone, in fact, who's apt to say,
"Because it's something I need to do."

The Poet

Whatever happened to Danny Blair?
He showed such promise in English class –
rhymed couplets, triolets, haiku and sonnets.
He would sit cross-legged on Mr. Barnes' desk
long after the others had gone,
mixing unexpected things with his talk
like "The half light of impending snow"
or "The sun seems to be stuck on noon,"
often laughing at his own words
since they always came as a big surprise.
If ever there was a lyrical mind it was Danny's.

And slowly, slowly, as he grew,
began to shave, his voice sounding deeper,
his poems mentioned some fictional Ruth
though we all guessed it was Marianne –
she at least a year older than we were.
"The dancing trees looked at them and smiled!"
He wrote as they lay by the drainage canal
or, on seeing Ruth through her bedroom window –
"She sitting before her mirror
training the mystery of her gender
by practicing seductive glares
or assuming provocative little poses."

But Danny finally became Mr. Blair –
suburban commuter, his briefcase a part of him
and that serious face... that faraway face.
Does he ever think of Marianne?
Did she tell him he's too young for her?
Or did someone say poetry's for the birds?
Sometimes he sits in Harry's Bar
jotting words in his pocket notebook.
Is he calculating the close cost of flour?
Or does he make notes about things around him?
"The flies are drunk on unfinished martinis
and wobble through the smoky air."
Or "She pierces me with her long green eyes."
Or "Shards of guitar chords lie on the floor –
all that remains of last night's party."

Maybe he owns a steel box
with a combination no one else knows,
just for hiding his little notebooks.
Because he is Chief Executive Officer
in charge of Agricultural By-Products,
lives in a house with a very long driveway
and seems content with the life he is leading,
so no one must know what's on his mind
or learn that once his life was all poetry,
that he used to sit on Mr. Barnes' desk
with his legs crossed, talking poetry... poetry.

Final Chapter

They should have used plastic garbage bags
to get rid of Aurelia's unfinished novels,
not this blazing bonfire last night,
this bone-fire of notebooks, this soul-fire of her,
this witches' Sabbath cremation of her.
But after all, it's a year since she died
and her room is still nothing but clutter.

Aurelia, secretly scribbling Aurelia,
all those novels no one had seen
trying to reveal her real self
in a hundred faces, a hundred names
with carefully chosen, building-block words
that could be held up for the world to see,
that could shout, "This is me, the real me!"
Though none of them quite like the real Aurelia.

Aurelia, writing her eyes away
puffy-eyed, blurry-eyed, red-eyed Aurelia,
bookworm Aurelia who looked at men
from behind the curtains of her eyes
she, the ultimate private person.
But each of her various characters
revealed herself as wanton and wild –
her tongue, her touch, her electric thighs.
Aurelia as Eve, the curved rib
plucked from the side of slumbering Adam.
Aurelia in fluffed-up, ruffled-up gingham
stretched out with her head in his lap,
the two of them humming "Edelweiss"
there on the river bank, love in their eyes.

This burning of all her unfinished novels
shoots flames of Aurelia up in the dark,
a swirling, unfurling silhouette
of sparkling, moon-soaked, mad Aurelia
tangled in love on various mattresses,
moon-bleached beaches or tall grass,
released from the mazes of her brain
until one slim, voluptuous puff of her
swirls up and over the trees.
"Goodbye, Aurelia!" to the vanishing smoke...
To the end of her novels – "Aurelia, Goodbye!"

My Uncle's Monocle

The poetry judge blows filtered smoke
on one more example of plodding iambics,
skims, scans, and frowns at the poem
as he tortures the 20-pound bond of its body
with his glowing cigarette,
leafs through the losers with serpentine fingers,
The Squirrel At The Window... My 3-Stringed Guitar...

"But where is the magic? What should I feel?
This intoxication of words makes me fly
from the gutter all the way up to the curbstone.
The syntax. The spelling. The imagery.
These people have nothing to say.
The Class Reunion... The Gypsy Singer...
immortalized in stilted pentameter.
Oh, Lord – Deliver me!

The mound of victims grows and grows,
My First Day At School... The Night Spot Died...
each condemned by a blue slash
to a bleak oblivion destiny,
each the fruit of a midnight candle
sprung from a random word in the blood,
from the voice of an afternoon almost forgotten
or the memory of a vanished face.

When this Judgment Day is over
only *Grammar School Dance* has survived,
shivering on the floor by itself
to be mailed with an autocratic remark
like "I have chosen this!"
While the others, the mountain of casualties,
are bulldozed into a mass grave
to level off an adjacent lot,
sprinkled with soil and seeded with Blue Grass
and biodegraded by sun and rain.

Until now, as the Great Authority sleeps,
his lips heralding every breath
there can be heard, often just before dawn
under the path of the wheeling moon
with day a thin sliver in the east,
a whisper more quiet than leprechaun singing
in the tall waving grass of the vacant lot,
the sound of faint little voices reciting
strange things like *My First Day At School*
or *The Squirrel At The Window*
or *The Night Spot Died*
until the wind in the giant catalpa
claps its leaves politely.

Mythical Creatures

Long after the last unicorn disappeared
it was said there had once been an animal
that looked like a cross between horse and gazelle
except for a long straight horn
that jutted from its forehead.
It liked to gently lay its head
on the laps of young maidens who sat in the forest
but became extinct when conniving hunters
dressed up like women would sit and wait
with daggers hidden beneath their skirts
and killed the noble unicorns.

And after the elephants disappeared
it was said there had once been an animal
with ears as large as window shades
and two large tusks it would sometimes use
to carry trees it had uprooted
with its hose of a nose that could also be used
to suck
up water from the river.

And after the last poet disappeared
it was said there had once been people
who would spend their lives stringing words together
talking their rhythms, dancing their rhymes,
making nonsense seem like reason
and logic like a drunk.
They would dream their apartments into palaces,
dream their poverty to wealth
while their children, hollow-eyed and hungry
prayed for some cure to be discovered
for this mania for words.

The Kidnapped Poem

Help!
He's gone!
His crib is empty!
There are ladder marks on the window ledge
and mud tracks on the rug.
Who could have done such a terrible thing?
Issue a bulletin right away –
he needs a special formula
and requires constant care.
Oh, what a beautiful one –
his sense of rhythm already apparent,
his little imageries seem so perfect
and such beautiful iambic feet.

The maid!
I really suspect the maid!
She's been acting very unusual lately,
speaking almost in whispers over the phone
and loitering by the gate with a strange man.
Oh, she's in on it, all right.
But be sure to leave a light in the window.
And a reward – offer a substantial reward.
No questions asked.
Oh, this is terrible –
I'll be searching poem faces forever.

Open Reading

The audience had gone on strike –
not planned... nothing prearranged,
just poof! At the very peak of a sonnet
they all got up and walked out of the hall
leaving Stanley, he of the resonant voice,
reciting iambics of three-legged dogs,
his sorrow for dying butterflies,
his love of Lorraine and her bouncing hair –
every work shining, his musical voice
reaching out to hold them back.

But the audience was already out in the night,
protesting along the neighborhood streets
about how unfair to have to listen
to dithyrambs of squirrels at the window
or the lonely white albatross lost in the city.
Forced to listen to Rosemary Jones
read from her book of gingerbread poetry
or Stanley booming his rhymed couplets.

But Stanley didn't care, or even notice,
just kept reading to empty chairs
about conjured-up flowers and dead trees
and the bones of desiccated fish,
things the audience never would hear –
flying horses leaving their nests
or uncaring women being sold as slaves.

Parts of the audience had gone
to their favorite restaurants to write on napkins,
discovering such things as June rhymes with moon.
Some sat by the banks of the sluggish canal
to watch the moon ripple over the water
and some danced in the empty streets,
their bells and tambourines jingling the air.
Some sat all night by their guttering candles
trying to give birth to some blank verse,
secretly planning to carve it in stone
unaware that Stanley, with no one to stop him,
was still reading poems in the empty hall.

On Dozing During A Poetry Reading

Everything was so normal –
the folding chairs, the busy woman
the rivery grain of the hardwood floor.
And the brief introduction, the polite applause.
Even the poet – his swarthy face,
his gold-tooth smile
neck veins pumping his slow pulse –
reeking of fresh air, brimming with meaning.
And his first line;
"Had I trained my tree from its sapling size..."
A beautiful line. I wish I had written it.

But then the loss of radar contact.
Different voices in my head. Dissonant music,
like psychedelic mushroom dreams
permeating my tower of sleep –
the anguish of a *viola da gamba*,
a flute creating shepherds and sheep.
And great unconscious revelations:
A film of chop suey clings to the trees!
Women have longer teeth than men!
The continents are shifting and no one cares!

And then Marie coming back from oblivion
Marie, my gymshoe-type love of the full blouse
humming some wistful runic tune, but old now,
one of the brittle little ladies
mincing daintily down the street
her freshness turned to eggshell white,

her perceptive eyes to chicken blink.
O Marie, stay away from the brittle ladies.
Come back as my galloping, gangly love.
But occasional metaphors seep through:
"Stars cling to the branches like bats."
Or, "An angelus of cowbells clanking."
Then applause, like hail on a galvanized roof
like a cheap clock's goading alarm
dredging me up from my lost dimension.
And a sharp pain in the right shin
dealt by all outraged poetry lovers
jolting me upright and wide awake.

I'm surprised by righteous indignation.
They know! They know! Everyone knows!
The poet smiles at everyone but me.
I must have breathed heavily... maybe snored.
My Lord! I'll be ostracized for good.
I'll move to an island. Move to the slums.

But being mature, being highly developed
I join the erudite coffee drinkers
acting civilized and aloof
ignoring their frowns of total outrage.
"Did you enjoy it?" I asked a young girl
who seemed less hostile than the rest.
"Frankly no. He's always been an insufferable bore."
Oh, I could hug that vacuous girl.
How alike we are in so many ways.

Poemectomy

The trouble was they left her too much alone,
feeding on books and dreaming of love
and watching willow trees shadows
sway across the polluted river.

Instead of running about and laughing
and talking of nothing with the other girls,
she grew wistful and wan and dangerously thin
and after hours on pondering such things as
frost on a window
or the frail filament fingers of an old nun on a bus
she would look weaker than ever
and complain of a terrible pain in her chest.

Until late one night when they rushed her to the hospital
and worked over her for hours in Emergency, removing a
huge, tumorous verse
so horrible that even the nurses grew sick when they saw it.
For days afterwards
she was draining words where the stitches were
and then only a few letters now and then
until finally the wound was completely healed.
But there's still a large scar where they made the incision
and even now when she sees things
like a bird on a twig
or the shadow of leaves on the sand
or a butterfly wing washed up on the shore,
the scar turns pink or a livid red
and you almost wonder
if they succeeded in getting out all the infection.

Poetry 1-A

Notice how
Miss Carruthers
carries her dead
poem, cradling it
in her arms. Can't
she see it isn't
breathing, that
its immediacy
is glazed over
and its rhythm
blotched? You
can tell by looking
at Miss Carruthers
she'd never
be able to nurse
it.. Doesn't
she know it
stopped crying
soon after it was
born? Someone...
please...
take it away from
her. It doesn't
even look like
her and Lord
knows who the
father was.
Make her give
it up.
Why should
we be sub –
jected to
this sort
of thing?

The Appraisal Of Days

Some days, when they die, are borne up by angels.
Others are buried, cranked into the ground
with no unctuous clergyman mumbling his nothings,
no honking of noses by the bereaved –
just sighs of relief that it's finally gone.
Seldom is anyone dressed in black.

Days are like children – sent off with a prayer
but you never know – they all turn out differently.
You instruct them, try to set an example
but often they grow up vicious and leave
after sheets are drawn over your murdered hopes.
Days have about the same life span as sand flies –
come out of nowhere and, like a parade,
disappear on the hazy horizon.

According to several criminal experts
there is no such thing as a bad day.
Yet some days seem irritating on purpose,
subjecting you to such puzzling things
as an unexpected face in a crowd
that bursts like a flower through the snow,
some face with a long history of solitude
hidden by undecipherable eyes,
some face that completely defies explanation.
You know you can't bury the dead day
until you understand this face
or else you'll carry it into tomorrow
because of this fantasy you have
that there has to be meaning in everything.

We decide which are good, decide which are bad
by what the day brings us – little or much,
pleasant or tragic, joyful or sad,
though good for you may be bad for me.
If every day were much the same –
coming from nowhere and fading to nowhere,
the sun would sweep over its empty world
and the stars would look down thinking barren is normal.

Confession

When I think of the time I have killed,
the days I have murdered,
some that died easily,
days like phlegmatic fish that were ready to die,
days like sluggish birds
that would otherwise have been prey for cats,
tired, exhausted days like ponderous, rotten trees
or old dogs with sleep in their bones.

But even vital and lively days I have murdered,
stepped up behind them when they were happiest,
at the peak of their vigor,
and slipped my knife of fine-tempered boredom
between their ribs
and watched with no emotion
as they slumped to the ground.

And often,
usually in the cold grey of winter
or when rain came as a depressing drizzle,
I would take a day up to my apartment
and we would have a snack and talk
and listen to music
and then we would stretch out on the studio couch
still talking and thinking
until I, sometimes against my will,
would hold a pillow over the day's face
until all breathing stopped.

Some days died hard –
days I would ply with liquor and bludgeon to death
or poison with special emotions I had developed.
Some I even starved to death,
locked them up in parlors of puritan Sundays
which became stone towers
with moats of abstinence around them
and let them rot with television and bridge.

The days of summer I treated most gently.
I would always choose one of exceptional beauty
and we would lie for hours on the warm beach
turning slowly, slowly,
facing the orange sun as it moved through the sky
and then, just before dusk,
I would suggest that we go out for one last swim
and we would step into the cool water
and wade past the breakers
and swim out, out past the sandbars and buoys
to a spot as deep green as dark moss
and we would tread water for a few moments
and look up at the first star
and then, as the last trace of color drained from the sky,
I would press the day's head down under the waves,
waiting until the bubbles stopped showing
before I could swim back to shore alone.

Of course there was some remorse at first,
in autumn with its anguish of leaves turning brown
or in winter with its finality of ice,
when I would think back with a sense of loss
for all the beautiful days I'd destroyed,
though lately such qualms no longer disturb me.

But I know I'm almost finished;
there is not much time left to kill
and there are fewer days that I care to murder.
Besides, I have been so careless with these crimes –
someone is certain to find the skeleton
of a murdered day wedged between the rocks
or the hand of a mutilated day
protruding from the ground
with some incriminating clue nearby,
like my glove or my comb or the print of my shoe,
and I will be apprehended at last
and locked up with days and days and days
that will sooner or later
torture me to death.

Rites Of Spring

It's April and I'm slowly turning green.
It's spring! It's here, and those who have
survived the winter of steam heat, chained
to their desks, shoes nailed to the floor,
seek out the sun and dance their dance
to unaccompanied flute.

Young bachelor girls keep swaying through the streets,
shed their winter clothes like last year's skin
innocently causing several traffic jams
while chlorophyll keeps rising in my veins.
Meanwhile Monarchs and other future butterflies
rattle about in their cocoons feeling it's time
to pollinate some flowers, and so far
several Greeks near Harrison and Halsted
have abducted acquiescent brides.

And from the platforms of their loading docks
young men of forehead horns and cloven hoof
yell springtime ritual propositions
to girls as thin as trees at timberline
who tap their pizzicato down the street,
filling out before your very eyes.
O spring... O whistling woman... O crowing hen,
the earth has swung to April once again.

About the Author

John Dickson lives in Evanston, Illinois. He is a former member of The Chicago Board Of Trade. He had his own grain trading business. His first volume of poetry Victoria Hotel received a Friends of Literature award in 1980. Waving at Trains was published in 1986 and Music Of Solid Objects was published in 1997. In 1971 he received first prize in Poesia Gradara, a poetry award sponsored by the Italian Government. In 1990 he received a grant from The National Endowment for the Arts. His poems have appeared in many journals and anthologies. He has received numerous awards including awards from, Poetry, Triquarterly, Poet Lore, Jean's Journal, and The National Federation of State Poetry Societies. He is the former Treasurer of Poets and Patrons, The Thorntree Press, and The Poets' Club of Chicago.

Also available from Puddin'head Press

PROPHECIES by Lawrence Tyler
THROUGH MY EYES by Samuel Blechman
I'M NOT TONIGHT by Kris Darlington
THE ANTI-MENSCH ANTHOLOGY
THE ANTI-MENSCH II ANTHOLOGY
JUST A SOUTH SIDE GIRL by Rose Virgo
professional cemetery by johnny masiulewicz
CONVERSATIONS WITH FRIENDLY DEMONS
AND TAINTED SAINTS by Nina Corwin
THRESHOLDS by Jeff Helgeson
LESSONS OF WATER AND THIRST by Richard Fammeree
CROWDPLEASER by Marc Smith
LADY RUTHERFURD'S CAULIFLOWER by JJ Jameson

and

WAVING AT TRAINS by John Dickson
MUSIC OF SOLID OBJECTS by John Dickson

For more information and a complete catalog call or write:

Puddin'head Press
P. O. Box 477889
Chicago IL 60647
(708) 656-4900